TO
MY NEPHEW,
LOVE FROM
....

Hi,
What's your
name?

On a normal street like yours and mine,
It was a bright and sunny day.
You opened the door, and suddenly saw,
A gang of animals waiting to play.

The tiger loves taking centre stage,
He's quite the confident one.
But equally, and I'm sure you'll agree,
His shy friends are also fun.

Let'sss play all day!

Hide-and-seek's a favourite game,
You're playing against the giraffes.
Your careful disguise won't fool their eyes,
And it ends with smiles and laughs.

Here we come,
ready or not!

Some friends like to relax and snuggle,
Others creep about and are tickly.
The otters hug, the gorillas are snug,
And the porcupines are cute and prickly.

Wanna hug?

The sloths love hanging out and snoozing,
While the monkeys swing about.
You cheerfully grin at the jumps and spins,
And the wild and cheeky shouts.

ZZZZZ

It's time to settle down for lunch,
Your burger takes some beating.
Your friends have FRUITS,

GRASS, GRUBS and ROOTS,

There's an icky stench wafting
through the air,
And you're slowly turning greener!
It might just be, the hippo, you see,

Or perhaps the
RING-TAILED
LEMUR?!

Oh no! The rhinos are squabbling!
They're bickering and butting their heads.
Your shouts didn't stop, their childish strop,
So you tried a spot of juggling instead.

Your hair is a little bit messy,
"But my friends look much funnier!"
you think.

They're BUSHY and BRISTLY,
SPIKY and FRIZZY,
All coloured red, orange
and pink.

Hooray! You've found a trampoline,

It's sure to raise a grin.

The giraffe takes flight,
And the hippo's a sight,
As they LEAP and

BOUNCE and SPRING.

Night night,
sleep tight

You're tired and ready to head back home,
As night eclipses the day.
But there's still time,
For a little more rhyme,
As your friends have
SOMETHING TO
SAY....

You're fun!
You're clever!
You're friendly!
You're kind!
You really love to play!

You just can't deny,
As you wave goodbye,

Now draw all your different friends and tell us why they're so special.

Written by Joe Barnes
Illustrated by Cinzia Battistel
Designed by Alice Xavier

First published by HOMETOWN WORLD in 2019
Hometown World Ltd
1 Queen Street
Bath
BA1 1HE

Visit
www.hometownworld.co.uk

Follow us @hometownworldbooks

ISBN 978-1-78979-142-6

Printed in Italy
HTW_PO201910

Hometown World